Corridor

Corridor

Josephine Singer

Borderland Books

Published by Borderland Books, Madison, WI
www.borderlandbooks.net

Publisher's Cataloging-in-Publication Data
Singer, Josephine.
   Corridor / Josephine Singer — 1st ed.

ISBN: 978-0-9768781-5-5

1. Title.
PS3619.I54 C67 2008
811/.6   2007924361

Printed in the United States of America
First edition

For my father

Contents

Corridor

Solution

The way up
and the way down
are the same

because it is always
you

just the one
pair of legs

the one eye

iterating
thoughts of the road.

Schedule

To see.

To work.

To be inscribed,

to be incised upon.

Then to read off

the inner epigraphy.

Terms

The light at the end
of the tunnel
is another tunnel
a narrower
and darker hole:

once the last of the days
of endurance
was a part of life

and now no end
but an endless
desert abutting the mountains.

They gave me
time and a sky
to welter over it.

The Fetus-Penis in the Weetabix

Fascinating
at one time.
Now the revelations
float a little in the air
and dissipate.

The secret is
amiable, old-fashioned:
quaint
even to have one.

And what matter where?

But the pulse
did move,
coursing
from that box to this,
dark to dark,

hitched corridors

into another
true recess.

New Year

We were cheerfully discussing the effects
of foreshortening. Party sounds tinkled
all around. The end of the century was near,
and the end of life, never that far away.
How nice to speak prose in a time of peril.
The pie gets bigger, as fewer of us
remain to share it. Hello, pie:
today we want to eat you up, it's a good day,
and tomorrow is yesterday with a frisson.
Give us our margin, whose shape is so
clean and clear, simply the plain road
leading on to its destination.

Twin Scourges

Is a waste of time really a waste?
How much of a waste is it, when
every little work has the sand
dribbling out of it like a bag
burst at the seam? How much
not wasted is the fruitful hour,
but how much not wasted is the
wasted hour? They are converging:
good, that opens the way to
a general slackening, to guilt-free rest,
though it's a kind of sleep in life,
ease achieved at the cost of draining
color out of the great idols,
stature out of the misty face.

Object

A thing comes into the house

and it might crumble

or it might survive you.

People arrive,

people in the extended family,

and they like it.

They say: "It's today's party dress."

"We know we're playing this scene in a vacuum."

Provision

I'm talking
but I'm wishing it was over.

Let's go back
to the bubble of the evening:
lamplight, homework,

the moment that enfolds itself

bends over itself
and smiles

dispelling
its complement.

It's good
though bare,

abbreviated,

a circle of ash,
and warm within.

I shall have it,
says the pilgrim,

where the light falls,

in place of utter nakedness.

The Marvellous Façade

1. Get up close to it
and it isn't there,

the mirage,
the disappearing act.

But there's no vacuum:

masses of reality
crowd in
to take its place

and why
should they seem
inferior

because you didn't want them?

2. How full
the world is

hanging lankly
from your hand.

3. The innate
ideas

were false
evidently:

strange to have them

to have been
beguiled by them

to honor them

in their absence and
irreality.

The Short Answer

what are they
but a stream of conversation

and I too
am conversing
enthusiastically

in my mind
with them

carousing
in talk
with these phantoms

who cannot love
or be loved.

Parade Without People

The festivities began in early morning.
The road, though empty, was strewn
with flowers. Dust blew round
and a soft breeze. It was the beginning
of summer. I heard nothing,
or maybe I heard the noise
of revelers, invisible, far
in the distance. The light changed.
clouds swung over the sky and
gave a little shade, and then
the blue darkened and it grew cold.

One must not wait any longer.

The whisper in the ear, the soft voice,
is an artifact of the corridor,
and the leap in the breath, always
practicing, prepares to no end,
as if lodged in us wrongly,
or crafted for another life.

Another Spanish Castle

True speech
and consummate answer

pacing at midnight
in broad day,

the shadow of one world
flung upon another,

a giant in the head
stalking the parapet

though unoccasioned
though unrealized
and unreal.

Harvest-Time

The last and then the last
of the last and then the last

of the last of the last:
this year we start to measure

because we finally have
measures enough: some things

are clearly finished
and the ones left are each

like a handful of sand:
one of everything,

the end in the beginning,
floor-samples:

this concludes our spurious
internal adventure:

though the ghost-avenues
led nowhere, they made

a finely-calibrated
anodyne, and how spare

the mirage without them:
mere furniture, white walls,

disembodied sound,
and not a soul in sight.

The Enormous Pivot

So nothing is
written in stone
in advance

but worse still
it is happening
right now

determining itself
fixing itself
so that

one moment
it is running
and the next

frozen
it is
what actually

happened
and we are so
oddly stationed

in respect of it
riding
the crest

unknowing
and then suddenly
all is known

as if it had
sat there to be known
forever

we anticipate
this anomaly

that what
has no being
at all now

will become
hard truth
in an instant

yet knowing
the structure
how it waves

in the wind
in its own form
gives one

no leverage
only the particulars
count

and they are
exactly
what can't be

predicted
what is held
in no hand

inscribed
nowhere
the chance

that is final
and always
a surprise.

The Surprises

Proverbs are true
but not quite
true enough.

They are exactly true.

It can all be
seen in advance

and not
for what it is.

A lonely life
is a whole

but that it should have
ellipsis points,

and spin
and trail

and transmute itself

recasting

the same form
in a different form,

and never rest,

that is
a flourish held back.

The End of Greatness

The map revealed galaxies glittering like bonfires in majestic arcs and filigree patterns hundreds of millions of light-years across, as well as vast regions called voids, and it confirmed a fundamental assumption about the birth of the universe: that cosmic structures have a maximum size, called the "end of greatness."

The New York Times, June 2000

Flung out to the farthest point
of the arc, now we're rounding back,
doubling the headland, and we've
seen it all, the whole of it
as one thing, large as experience
gets, the complete continent
of happiness, as far as it goes.

Effect

Everyone is sure of silence
but maybe not
the silence of silence.

Strangely the waves,
which had disappeared,
again and again,
day after day, lost their
dark blue mass.
They moved as light as air.
They could not slap nor sway.

And so it was:
a deeper grade
turned round
into a surface and

made the surface
final.

Plutonium Wind

The wind goes backwards
irradiating
the forms in their tableaux,

blazing them
as they
hold their shape in ash

and then collapse.

There was nothing
but these forms.

Now, the one
black point.

Thumomancy

The courtyard is lined with dirt.

Creepers
break the stone.

This rubble
stays,

it's here to stay,

smudging the air,

intertwined

with daylight.

Want a clean breath?

You seem
to have had them

but these

meet bedrock
halfway down.

Guesswork

Grainy dark

warm air

all around and

not to know

where the break is

or which kind.

Failure

It could be
like this:

an asymptote
never reaching the line,

a long
low arc.

Teleology

Well now, what is no longer

amassing toward an end

might be flooding

the lateral plains

smearing finality's

golden burr

over the quirks of day

dear mortal things

but as we declare

that it does so

the voice fails

a hollow gapes

under the affirmation

it is spread too thin

over the change it has to cover

no, we do not

believe it

the world

wavers

it cannot

commend itself.

In Flight

Why shouldn't it be now

seeing as there is
no shape after all

but a billowing sail

and the sucking
breath of the wind?

The Phantom Equation

Casting a line

out in the water

waiting

surely this is

not the right way

to experience

time

what is this

waiting

postponement

delay

oh

some things

you have in your hand

soon enough

and

of those

we need never speak

it is

the waiting

that at first seems

temporary

then slowly

reveals itself to be

unending

that insists

on being honored

in spite of being

manifestly vain

it is

the dawning sense

you have

what you

most passionately

wanted all along

will never come to pass

in the midst of

everything

always too much

coming to pass

and yet you cannot

stop waiting

you cannot

suspend your wish

and now you are

caught yourself

on the line

snared

fighting

the hook

fast in the flesh of

indissoluble

longing

made sharper

now it is clear

the days will

never add up to it

fierce little

tongue of iron

spearing

the soft place

in the heart

this is the

expense of time

See For Yourself

From a distance

it looks like

sprinting across the field

why do they flounder

but on the field

the feet stick

they come up with

long

retarding

glutinous bands

and everything

slows down

radically

it is

hard to progress

as in a dream

obstacles

that seem

trivial from afar

upend

and they are

steep slopes now

surmounting

a root in the earth

is cause for

celebration

or three steps over

the embattled ground

and we applaud ourselves

but with

ulterior contempt

it was a thing

of no account

once.

Continuity

The tinsel is tinsel
after all, and the heart is still
silence.

      Across the border,
the grandstands fill.

      We shall not
come out of this fog,
nor is there any need to:

night arrives from under it,
and sits down satisfied.

Hoc

Certain how one
merely
alights
upon the world

how
like a dimpling of the water

there will be no
gap

and the living
will

do what the living do,

then one sees
the light and the dark
in two clean halves,

and the dark is true

and the truth is over.

After the Fact

It is birth
that confirms
mortality.

How easily
a new mind
is made

how readily
it springs
into the world

riding
so light

it cannot
have been made
to stay.

Half-Circle

coming forward in the flame

outlines

professing life

melting

into the flame

The River God

To lose oneself
completely

is not permitted

and after the ends
have dissolved,

what to do with the salience?

I try

losing it
at the next level up.

But there's a tug.

There are thick, waving
reeds below,

all that was
meant once

and cannot be forgotten.

Drift

specifically

sand

dry sand

and the way it moves

easily

lightly

covering

something over

bright day

sweet breeze

I went on

failing to see

how the grade

softened

how the hollows

filled in

I came out of my trance

doubtfully

having forgotten

having been

comforted

and liking

where I was

in spite of falsehood

older depths

circled up

dark

into light water

I was guilty

but still

I admired

forgetfulness

Defeat By Life

Be careful:

metaphors already abound

the bowed head
the sunken hope

nonetheless
I want to

say it again
in my own way

or any other.

It does not lose
its fascination,

so strong it is,
such a prince.

Deferral

Today is a veil.

When it goes

opaque

then

that is happiness.

And is it

forgetting

is that the right word?

Blocking

it out,

not-seeing?

(Well we try

but it can't be

counted on.)

Or else it's

what's real

and the rest of life

thought

spinning out

over time

is false,

superfluity.

But is it possible?

Craving

the cradle of the sunlight

today

today

nestled in its hollow,

we are not free:

dark air

sways the curtain

whatever is there

shows

what is left out

and the seeping is

hard to staunch.

If it's

sheer oblivion

you want

there are

plenty of ways

to find it

but you want

an experience

quiet

tropical

unselfconscious

yet

conscious of itself

not an antonym

having the character

of its own denial

rare magic

is it possible?

Say it is.

Say we say it is

despite the price:

deferral,

the long

twisting

gap

between reprieves.

It Takes Summer

It takes summer
to cross the path
with a bar of light

to
fix the contrast:

pleasures wave
like seaweed

they make you think
of happiness

they say
it is alright

here
where we are

And the more
beguiling
they are

the more they
oscillate.

Oblivion
is an effort

And the effort
remembers the lie.

When A Surface Is Divine

The eye lights

and the touch

and the greed light

upon the things of this world.

The joy of them

is ill at ease

changeling

in the bed of dreams

yet it

tilts back up

fluttering

when the ballast

of a larger life

is gone.

In the Time Allotted

Clearly
it is not enough

and the more
you know of it

the more you see
how far short

it must fall:

the paint
overflows the canvas

sacks open and
decant
the bright stuffs,

how much deeper
into the glory
one may get

into the crevasse
where
riches lie,

even to be here
one more year

doing the same things
over again

seems nice

but that was not the point:

there is a scheme
and in it

joy is
a brush of the wingtip,

accidental.

Maniples, Centuries, Cohorts
and Legions

Since every other
avenue
is cut off

all roads
lead inward.

The doors standing open
to let in light

let in
cold gusts now

rubbish
scuttles across the floor.

Climb high
into the aerie of your own head

the hospice

the quiet box where

mere fact
is to be found.

Skewered Economy

Yet at times it is

completely sufficient.

Allurements

wither

and the light

darts inward

like a shrinking

drop.

The dreadful faces

and the fiery arms.

Return.

Contract.

There: the innermost room

radiant

invisible square

of

freedom

in which to be

confined.

Historical Atlas

The dead world
to sink into

willingly:

ready to stop
prayer

now

to ask

nothing
for oneself.

Constraint

The illusion

of moving freely

unfolding the arms

and turning the body

each way

in the unresisting air

breaks

from time to time

or else

becomes a dream

when it is broken

reminders

alight

seizings

and the image is reversed

bound tightly

unresting

driven on in

labor without consent

to liquefy the days

and watch them falling.

Death of a Thousand Cuts

The body goes

in jumps

and in small increments

and so goes

the soul

one

joy at a time

in jagged bursts

and in insensible

erosions

grain

by grain

so that we see

in stages

how to make do

with less

how to make

less

seem roomy

or

shape the soul

so that it needs

less room.

One Autumn

The yellow tree
in the cup
is today's portion

the child
smiling

just for today

it is day
it is happiness
that undoes itself

it bears
its overcoming
so frankly
in its face.

Little One

Little one
I cling to you

and I give way
to the illusion

eternal
unmoored island

glass-roofed
admitting sun

and we two.

But it is hard
in fact
to secure the line

to contain

seepage

the moment is leaking

prospects
trickle in

and the illusion wobbles.

It wobbles
it sways
it holds
halfway

like any bounded light.

Table Wine

The revelation of the rose
is incremental,

a function:

take half and divide that half
in half
and take that half…

steadily
a little smaller,

somewhat less

but not wholly
given over.

We take
what they give us,

bread in an open hand.

Condensation

Films
fallen away
one by one

we are down to
the generic self

moving
and lamenting
as others do

knowing it is
representative

a small thing
clear like water.

Story and Ashes

The wide air
is invisible.

Night flows
everywhere,

into each corner.

I who am
so light

see the masters

pouring in
filling the shoal

with life.

A Hard Winter and a Cold Spring

Something else chooses.

Then motion is strange:

to go forth
while standing still,

to make the slight
but laborious gestures,

rowing
long after night falls
and the wind is gone.

Few Words

Everywhere comfort

is being given

People are talking

in their beds

on the street

in restaurants

Some put out one hand

some caress

and they are saying

true things

showing

true kindness

as between

one soul and another

Outside

the stars are

hot and real

they burn

whatever words are said

and the wind

vaults

over the house

the murmur

going on

out into the night

unheard

is one half

of the broken

promise.

Fewer Dreams of Flying

They have done it

before us

and now

it is our turn

here we are

knowing and being

known to know

what cannot

be known otherwise

than by being here

where distance

slides

into the foreground

from our view

up front

but a long way off

from those

standing and looking

it is our turn to be

half-known

to carry and **sustain**

like

invisible pillars

to go blank

because we must

it is our turn

Ceremony

to begin again

to begin again

this time knowing

nothing will come of it

if it must

it must

be done

for its own sake

like the sand

mandala

we will

take it in our hands

we will

pour it all

into the river

knowing if not

it will

fly

to the river

in its own way

Low to the Ground

In the end

you'll

have to look

at what you

can see

as the long arcs

get shorter

and what lies

before you

grows larger

though

disdained

though it has been

help cheap

we know now

we will not

see farther

than the next rise

it has to do

it has to post

its own

glory.

Shifting Servitudes

After all

life

does not rise

above

a certain height

and the vigil

over the summit

must

come to an end

in our

learning to love

our grottoes

with their

uncertain light

and there the vigil

begins again

this time

to learn

love

for what was once

the road

the means

the dust

and now

is all there is

of the mansion.

The Sparks Fly Upward

Unfree when young

and like shifting

weight from

one foot to the other

older and still

unfree

but with new

discriminations

did some

go free

was it just us

or is there

one law for everyone

shall we add

self-reproach

to the summary?

(See how the closed system

fans firelight.)

Reverse Arrows

Quiet

is not a prospect

now

it does not

extend

into the distance

over the desert hills

it has been

turned back

pressed back

into this

modest room

where we sit

aiming for patience

trying to treat

motion as rest

and flight as

eternity

grasping

what is here

in this room

and trying

not

to grasp it

because we cannot know

when it will

arrive again

or if it is

here

for the last time.

Bergweg

Walk

up the mountain

slowly

come to the tree-line

and keep on going

up unto the dry

undifferentiated slopes

and climb on

toward the uninhabited

crown

time

has been such a mountain

to us

a falling-away

an accumulation

of strippings

and their replacement

by something as subtle as

dust and air

hard work

strange

weatherings

invisible

reacclimations

a thinning-out

which concentrates

attention

on the remaining leaves

reversing

brown to green

small to great

and the indifferent

to the last joy.

The Count

The things that are

still good

are few

but they seem

more real

now than at the time

when the world

billowed

with excellence.

It was a

recurrent theme of story –

they told us

again and again –

how treasures would

dissipate

one by one

to be replaced with

junk

and still we were

amazed

to find ourselves

at last

in the midst of junk.

It was arduous

to live it out

in one's own time

And falling into the story

did not help

no

it did not help to see

it was true and we

secretly hoping

to be spared

had become

the next example.

But the other truth

somehow

harder to tell

is true too

the few things

that are still good

condense

they become

harder

and brighter

ascending at last

into an actual

radiance

they never had

in the midst of cloud

putting on

substance and eternity

arcing

like warmth and light

in a distant window

rare

and therefore certain.

Debriefing

We weren't able to charge the gates:
at the last moment, a sudden flagging,
and each of us, musing, turned away.
In the group portrait, everyone looks
straight into the camera with an
impenetrable face. The hill was high,
it was spring, and some small yellow flower
ran up and down the slope. One journeys
a long way and the battle is not there.

This book is set in Adobe Garamond, a digital interpretation by Robert Slimbach of the sixteenth-century roman types of Claude Garamond and the italic types of Robert Granjon. It was designed by Ken Crocker. The book was printed at The Stinehour Press, and bound by Acme Bookbinding.